Coming Home To God

9/9/04

To Bobby & Eleanor,

With many thanks for your
gracious hospitality.

Palmer

John 12:24

Coming Home To God

by

O. Palmer Robertson

 EVANGELICAL PRESS

EVANGELICAL PRESS
Faverdale North Industrial Estate, Darlington, DL3 0PH,
England

Evangelical Press USA
P. O. Box 825, Webster, New York 14580, USA

e-mail: sales@evangelicalpress.org

web: www.evangelicalpress.org

First published 2003

British Library Cataloguing in Publication Data available

ISBN 0 85234 538 0

Scripture quotations in this publication are from the Holy Bible,
New International Version. Copyright © 1973, 1978, 1984, International Bible Society. Used by permission of Hodder & Stoughton,
a member of the Hodder Headline Group. All rights reserved.

Scripture quotations not taken from the New International Version
are the author's translation from the original text.

Printed and bound in Great Britain by
Creative Print & Design Wales, Ebbw Vale

Contents

Introduction:
The Eternal Plan

God has a plan. He must have a plan for this world and all the people in it. He would not be God if he did not have a plan. Birds make plans when they build nests. People make plans before they take a trip. God made this entire world, so he must have a plan for the world.

But what is his plan? What is his purpose for this world? Sometimes things seem so confusing. On the one hand this world is marked by such beauty. But clearly the world as God made it has been marred. It is defaced by ugly murders, incurable diseases, ruthless tyrants and internecine wars. How can such divergent things as beauty and bestiality exist side by side in this one world?

Living in this complex world, people proceed to make their own plans. Sometimes they plan beautiful, constructive projects. They design parks with lakeside walks and children's playgrounds even though we often see these good plans spoiled by litter, graffiti and vandalism. People also plan ugly, destructive things that are unpleasant to mention. They plan wars of aggression, they devise schemes to make themselves wealthy without adequate regard for anything else in God's creation. They consider their own race, their distinctive tribe, and their particular family to be the chosen, the favoured one. They conclude that all good things in the world should belong to them. As a consequence, they take aggressive actions to claim what they regard to be theirs by right.

So how do these two planners relate to one another? At first it would seem that the realms of God and men diverge so widely from one another that they must be seen as wholly unrelated. God and mankind seem to live in separate spheres, even though the objects of their concern often coincide.

But instinct tells you something should be different. Something inside you says the God who made you is not so far away. Somehow you sense that your realm and his rule intertwine, overlap, cover the same territory. Although you don't think about it all the time, nevertheless the sense of his involvement with your life is never absolutely absent from your instinctive understanding of the world in which you live.

You can trust your instincts, for your relationship to the invisible, intangible God actually is much closer than people sometimes suppose. In the original order of the world, Adam and Eve belonged to God as a son and a daughter in his home. Some intimations of that original order may come to you here and there, but you may have trouble retaining the awareness for any length of time – and for good reason. For the thing that once might have been has slipped through humanity's fingers, and has eluded them ever since.

But there is a way back. There is a coming home to God. All the warmth and pleasure associated with home-coming may characterize this event of re-establishing intimacy of relationship with God, the source of all that is life to you.

How does it happen? What can be done? Is returning home to God really worth the trouble it might bring into your life? Will you be able to maintain a sane attitude toward your job, your recreations, your time with people close to you? Will they sense something strange about you? Will they conclude something has gone wrong with you if you find yourself going home to God?

Never mind. Don't worry. God has a plan. He has a way of working out all the details for those who come home to him. The important thing at this very moment is for you to open yourself to the prospect that the process already has begun for you to come home to God.

In his parable about two sons, Jesus describes the way people come home to God. As you read this story in the following paragraphs, see how it may have significance for your life. Jesus said:

'There was a man who had two sons. The younger one said to his father, "Father, give me my share of the estate." So he divided his property between them.

'Not long after that, the younger son got together all he had, set off for a distant country and there he squandered his wealth in wild living. After he had spent everything, there was a severe famine in that whole country, and he began to be in need. So he went and hired himself out to a citizen of that country, who sent him to his fields to feed pigs. He longed to fill his stomach with the pods that the pigs were eating, but no-one gave him anything.

'When he came to his senses, he said, "How many of my father's hired men have food to spare, and here I am starving to death. I will set out and go back to my father and say to him: 'Father, I have sinned against heaven and against you. I am no longer worthy to be called you son; make me like one of your hired men.'" So he got up and went to his father.

'But while he was still a long way off, his father saw him and was filled with compassion for him; he ran to his son, threw his arms around him and kissed him.

'The son said to him, "Father, I have sinned against heaven and against you. I am no longer worthy to be called your son."

'But the father said to his servants, "Quick. Bring the best robe and put it on him. Put a ring on his finger and sandals on his feet. Bring the fattened calf and kill it. Let's have a feast and celebrate. For this son of mine was dead and is alive again, he was lost and is found." So they began to celebrate.

'Meanwhile, the older son was in the field. When he came near the house, he heard music and dancing. So he called one of the servants and asked him what was going on. "Your brother has come," he replied, "and your father has killed the fattened calf because he has him back safe and sound."

'The older brother became angry and refused to go in. So his father went out and pleaded with him. But he answered his father, "Look! All these years I've been slaving for you and never disobeyed your orders. Yet you never gave me even a young goat so I could celebrate with my friends. But when this son of yours who has squandered your property with prostitutes comes home, you kill the fattened calf for him!"

'"My son", the father said, "you are always with me, and everything I have is yours. But we had to celebrate and be glad, because this brother of yours was dead and is alive again; he was lost and is found."'[1]

Several truths in Jesus' parable deserve special consideration. Note first, 'The Wearisome Way.'

Bible References

Reference 1 is found in
Luke chapter 15 verses 11-32.

1
The Wearisome Way

The first evidence that you may have wandered far from God but now are ready to come back to him, may be found in the fact that life has become wearisome to you. You sense that life should not be so tiresome. Emptiness, aloneness, makes you think. This condition strikes different people in different ways.

Some people have it relatively easy in this life. They may have inherited property, position and prominence. By their early thirties they are already well established with a nice house, a satisfying job and an enjoyable family life.

But despite it all, something is missing. A hollowness, an emptiness, a vacuum fills the soul. They would give it all up, as many have done, if only they could understand the point of it all. 'Frustration of frustrations, frustration of frustrations, all is frustration,'[1] said the wisest man in the world. That was the estimate of life offered by King Solomon, even as he experienced all the abundance that life could offer.

Is that you? Have you had it relatively easy in life? Did you breeze through school, get a good job, enjoy early success, yet are you now feeling an inner emptiness? If you have it all and are content, then more's the pity. If you value the things of this world more than you value the Maker of the world, you will end up with neither the Maker nor anything he has made.

Not everyone, however, has such an easy way through life. You may be the kind of person who has had to struggle for every advantage. You were born in circum-stances that promoted low self-esteem. You had to hold down a menial part-time job to get through school or college. Your grades suffered because you were compelled to divide time between work and study. The only way you could find a permanent job was to give up the prospect of doing the kind of thing you really enjoyed. Since then you have had to struggle constantly to maintain basic housing and adequate clothing. All of life has been one endless struggle.

But every now and then you come up for a breather. You find a quiet moment. Then the questions come. What's the point of it all? Must you always struggle? Does life have lasting meaning?

Or you may fall into still a different category. Perhaps you are the kind of person who has no time for people who cry in their own cup. Life is simply something you *do*. Don't worry so much about it. Just do it! Work a little, play a little, stay on the upbeat, enjoy yourself when you can, and don't think about it when you can't. Don't waste your time looking for the 'missing something' because it probably doesn't exist.

If you have this kind of view about life, you're like the white-water rafter enjoying himself on the upper Zambesi in southern Africa. You enjoy the excitement of turbulent water. You can take it if you're bumped out of the boat. You also can enjoy the calm pools along the way, where the overhanging trees shade the riverbed. You take it all in your stride.

But little do you know that the thunderous Victoria Falls are just around the next bend. Your blasé attitude to life is based on a fantasy world that ignores the hard facts. One day your life may be shattered. Your spirit will sink. You may be forced out of home and job. Your family may leave you. Your daughter may run off with a drop-out or the doctor may explain that you have an incurable illness.

Is that you? Are you drifting pleasantly through space and time, never considering the fact that everything and every circumstance in this life has its ending-point? The tolerable surroundings of today may quickly give way to the inescapable distresses of tomorrow.

It's true, isn't it? Your way can become wearisome. The uphill struggle can get to you.

So it may be good news to learn that there is something
that may be designated the 'irresistible call'. The God who
made you is calling you, and for you his call may be
irresistible.

Bible References

Reference 1 is found in
Ecclesiastes chapter 1 verse 2.
The translation is from the original text.

2
The Irresistible Call

Sometimes in life a proposal confronts you that simply cannot be resisted. This proposal may come as the invitation of a friend to take you out to dinner at your favourite restaurant. Or it may come as a 'suggestion' from your boss that you spend the next Saturday at the office preparing materials for the company's annual report to the Board of Directors. The call, whether welcome or not, may be termed 'irresistible'.

From still another perspective, your 'irresistible call' may come in terms of a summons to jury duty or a notification from your government that your tax bill is overdue. In such cases, the 'authority factor' outweighs all other considerations. Your preference, your convenience, plays a very small role in your response to the summons when it comes.

The Deity has his own way of summoning people to himself. The circumstances can vary as widely as one human personality diverges from another. God called Moses at the end of forty years of obscurity living in the desert. The call came through a bush that burned but was not consumed. Moses thought God had forgotten all about him and his people. But the Lord had a time-schedule involving many peoples and nations. When the call came, Moses was ready even though he did not believe it at the time. He would have been unprepared at any earlier hour.

God called Isaiah through a revelation of his divine glory that shook the foundation of the temple of Solomon and set the prophet trembling. His call exposed Isaiah's utter moral bankruptcy and unworthiness to serve. But through his own limitless resources God supplied all things necessary for the prophet to endure the tough task ahead of him.

Andrew, Peter and Matthew received a call they could not resist in a less spectacular way. But the call came through the most spectacular of persons. As he walked along the lakeshore, Jesus indicated that two brothers in the fisherman's trade should submit to a re-tooling which would deploy their skills in a different way. They would begin fishing for men. Matthew had been exacting taxes from people, but now he found himself called to give a free gospel to rich and poor alike.

Can you sense the irresistible call? Could it be coming to you? How can you tell whether or not God is calling you?

First of all, know that God is calling all who truly want to come to him. That's simple enough, isn't it? If in your soul you want to come to God, then he is calling you to himself. Right now the Almighty may be addressing his invitation directly to you.

'Come to me, all you that are tired and troubled, and I will give you rest'.[1] Jesus said it. It's God's invitation to you. To be sure that you aren't frightened or overawed by an approach of the Almighty, the invitation to God comes from the God-man. As Immanuel, 'God with us,' this unique man named Jesus came into the world as a guarantee that God wanted people, even broken, burdened, self-deceived, self-indulgent people, to come to him.

So the call comes to you. Even if you cannot remember hearing it before, you have heard it now.

But obviously this call is not necessarily an irresistible call for everyone. It comes to 'all', but all do not come. You might not come. You might decide right now that you will not move from where you are. You will not change your settled patterns of life, and you will not submit to God's call.

On the other hand, the call may come to you as an irresistible force. You may find yourself wondering, 'How could anyone *not* come to God when he calls?' The call to come home to God may be so strong for you that resistance is not even a consideration. God has commissioned his son

Jesus to come and call people home to himself. At great price, Jesus has cleared the way. He has fulfilled all the appointments God made for him. He was the designated saviour of people who had a deep need to be brought back to God. As a consequence, certain obligations were laid on him.

Jesus lived a perfect life. He kept all God's commands from childhood, through the troublous times of youth, and to the end of his adulthood. This 'right-living' he did for people like you, so that his good life might be regarded by God as though it were yours. He died an undeserved death, a cruel, unjust, disgraceful death on a cross as a criminal. He died this death that you might not fear the separation from God that would come to you in your own death. By coming home to God through entrusting your life to him, you show that you will not, you cannot resist his call. Instead, you will gladly embrace the invitation to come to Jesus. You will trust him as the provision of God for needy people.

Jesus talked about this call in the story of the two sons. One son heard the call and came home. The other son heard the call quite clearly to come inside for a celebration, but had major problems. He found it difficult to accept the call.

You've seen situations like that, haven't you? One member of a family comes home to God, but another member never does. So this situation in Jesus' story should not be surprising. The surprising thing is who comes and who doesn't; who hears a call he cannot resist, and who is called but does not come.

Surprise! It's not the 'good' son who comes home. No. He refuses to enter the house of his Father even though he hears a party going on right then. He will stand outside. He will scowl and stomp his foot like a spoiled child. He supposes that he knows a better way to run his Father's household than the Father himself. So he'll stand outside on his own, even though he can see that those who have come into the Father's house are enjoying life *so much more*. No, the 'better' brother isn't the one who finds the Father's invitation irresistible. He is strong in himself. He can make it through this life on his own. He has good reasons for not saying 'yes' to his Father's invitation.

But the younger brother cannot resist. He's down and out. He has large needs. He's filthy dirty and has no place to wash himself. He's starving for a good dinner, but can't get enough cash for a single meal. He has lost all his partying friends because he's broke. That's when he gets the idea. He'll go home.

'He comes to himself.' That's the way Jesus describes the call that cannot be resisted. This brother suddenly realizes the potential involved in sonship to God. He will go home to God. Once the concept takes shape in his mind, it's all over. He has no more decision to make. He's going home to God.

Has the idea struck you yet? Is the call coming to you? Do you see the new dimensions of life that would be yours if you came home to God?

Jesus didn't tell this story of the two brothers for nothing. He told it so you could understand the difference. The invitation to come home to God is an open one. It's available to you as well as to everyone else. Some decide to resist the call. They won't enter the house of their Father even though they can see the bounties of life with God that others enjoy. They will stand alone, they will make it on their own. But others find the call to come home irresistible. They will not stay as they are. When Jesus says, 'Come to me, all you that are tired and troubled,'[1] they can't resist his call. They come. They enter the Father's house. They find their sins forgiven and the losses of life restored.

So how is the call to come home to God striking you? Are you resisting? Will you say no? Do you find the call to come back to God quite resistible? It's a pity if you do. The banquet table for abundant blessing in life is set, and you have God's own invitation to come home through Jesus his son. It would be sad if you kept finding in yourself the strength to say no.

But then you might be like the other son. You might say your life has been empty long enough. You've had enough hollowness. You hear Jesus Christ offering an open door to the Father's home, and you find his call irresistible.

You've got to come home to God right now. You will delay no longer.

If that's the way you're thinking, then come on! The Father has been waiting patiently for this moment. Deep down in your heart, where the Spirit of God speaks, say 'yes' to his summons. Embrace right now the offer of Jesus. Let his good life serve as your righteousness before God. Let his death substitute for the death you deserve for your departures from the Father's will. Let the Son who lives forever at God's right hand serve as your great intercessor with his Father.

The call comes. For you it may be irresistible.

Bible References

Reference 1 is found in
Matthew chapter 11 verse 28
The translation is from the original text

3

The Turning of Head and Heart

If a person will return to God, there must be a change of direction. How could it be otherwise? If you want to keep on going along through life on your own steam, then just keep on as you have been. You've been going this way a long time, and you can keep it up until the day you drop. Just keep on as you are, and you'll bypass God altogether.

But enough of this self-reliant philosophy. You can use both hands to grab the back of your heels, but you will only be able to pull yourself up so high. As a matter of fact, by tugging and yanking, by huffing and puffing, you won't even get yourself off the ground. You'll stay earthy forever, and that will be your undoing. For 'dust you are, and to dust you shall return'.[1] God pronounced these words as a curse on the first man after he decided to go it on his own, and the same curse continues right up to today.

But people are made for more than grovelling in the dirt. In the hands of the Redeemer they have great potential.

God has planted eternity in the human heart, and so we think, reason, and we come up with long-lasting concepts. We form ideas, and then by forcing a little wind across the tongue, teeth and lips, we speak first to ourselves and then to others. We capture a little air in our mouth, and by shaping wind into words, change the face of the world.

Through the way in which we form these ideas and words, a person attests that he is God-like. We even make ourselves into a god. And therein arises the need for change, for a turning of head and heart.

With their own inherent powers people make themselves into little gods. Very early they discover that they can bring other things (even other people) into the orbit of their ideas so that a certain amount of control can be exercised over them. People enjoy this feeling. They like the results. The little world around them becomes *their* world. Their brother's toys become their toys. With a little whimper they can make their mother's arms and legs work for them. Then the roads of the city in which they live become their roads, and the business contacts on the computer screen are theirs. Time and space are theirs. Things are 'right' when they are right for them, and if they are not working for them, then somehow they must be made 'right.' Every object they encounter may not yield immediately to their will, but the desired direction is quite clear.

But if there is only one God who has one will, then for all people there must be a change of head and heart. Coming home to God means setting a new direction for your life. Like a ship in the ocean, you have been pointing in one direction across the waves. But now you must make a mid-course correction so that all the energies of your life point in another direction.

A ship in the middle of the ocean appears as a mere speck on the sea. Its progress may seem minuscule. But every ship at sea has a set course. The vessel's course takes it from one continent to another. By a shift of the small, unseen rudder, the ship changes course so that it points to an entirely different continent. Eventually the difference will amount to hundreds of miles, and the destination may be Canada instead of Cuba, or the English Channel instead of the Mediterranean.

So the turning back to God happens inside the head and the heart. It's a step of faith that you must take. But take it. Go ahead. People from all across the ages will tell you that you will never regret it. God himself offers the greatest guarantee by the oath he has sworn. Either you trust his word, or you despise his oath.

But what does this turning involve? How must head and heart be re-directed?

First of all, the head must reject outright the view of this universe that begins by closing out God as an active agent in the course of men and nations. The scientific mindset, despite all the good it has done for us, has brought with it the plague of spiritual impoverishment. The world of science deals only with the material dimension of reality. Only what can be seen, heard, counted or measured is taken into account.

But God is pure spirit. He exercises more influence on this earth than the life-sustaining rays of the sun or the gravitational pull of the moon. As a matter of fact, he sustains these other powerful influences each moment of the day. Because of his invisibility, he never will be seen. Yet as a consequence of his immensity, he is always everywhere in his fullness as God. Apart from his continual infusion of power, the energy of the sun and the pull of the moon would cease to exist.

The mind must turn. It must release itself from the restrictions of the creation and embrace the vastness of the Creator. By faith you must turn your mind around so that you affirm the reality of the person of God.

This turning of the mind also must embrace the 'good news', the stupendous reality of the gospel message. God has been clothed in human flesh by the virgin birth of Jesus, his eternal Son. He became man to identify with people who had missed the mark of living for God. His undeserved death and transforming resurrection made it possible for human mortality to be exchanged for present and future immortality. 'Since by one man's disobedience (i.e. Adam's) death came through sin, so also by another man's righteousness (i.e. Christ's) came resurrection from the dead'.[2]

These truths your mind must embrace – and your heart as well. You have a centre for yourself, a 'distilled essence' of your being that crystallizes all the direction of your life. Your will, your emotion, your deepest reactions find their point of energizing in your 'heart' – not the physical organ of the chest, but the inner essence of your being.

In coming home to God, you cannot make your return on the basis of your own convenience and personal worth. He is God! You are only a frail creature of dust. He knows all about you, inside and out. He knows the lust of your flesh, the lust of your eyes, the pride of your life. For these sins of the heart you must repent. You must repudiate every bit of self-righteousness and ask for mercy on the basis of the merit of Jesus Christ alone.

So you must come with open confession of the sin of your soul. You must come wholly without reservation, recognizing that you deserve his condemning judgement and trusting his mercy alone for your salvation. It's the only way to come back to God.

This turning of head and heart also demands trust. You can never please God if you don't trust him. Don't bother coming home if you are not ready to entrust your entire life to him. He simply cannot and will not accept you on a lesser basis.

You do understand, don't you? The intimacy of the marriage relationship demands trust. Close friendship requires mutual trust. Any meaningful relationship rests on accepting a person for who they are.

It should not be surprising that God requires no less. Only in his case, accepting him for who he is means entrusting the whole of your life to his sovereign will. It means committing yourself to accept good and ill as coming from his hand. It means acknowledging that everything good in life comes from him, and that everything bad in life is still under his control and ultimately will work for your good and his glory.

Coming home to God is a good thing to do. Do it now. Turn your head and your heart to God. Recognize the self-centred disorientation of your life up to this point and repudiate it. Engage God with your mind and turn over the centre of your life to him.

Then you'll be at home with God.

Bible References

Reference 1 is found in
Genesis chapter 3 verse 19
NIV translation

Reference 2 is found in
Romans chapter 5 verse 19
The translation is from the original text

4

The Magical Moment

Don't get the wrong idea. God is not altogether passive in this interchange. You're coming home to God. But he's coming out to meet you.

How touching is the picture painted by Jesus in the story about the return of the son that had strayed from home. The son comes to his senses. He begins the long trek home.

But 'while he was still a *long way off*, his father saw him and was filled with compassion for him. He ran to meet his son, threw his arms around him and kissed him'.

Everything cannot be presented in a story. The nature of the literary medium prevents a succinct, accurate representation of all sides of a person's coming home to God. A story would have to be like one of Picasso's paintings to give the full picture, with multiple perspectives on the same event that occurs in a single moment of time. But then the story would appear as a barely understandable abstract.

It may prove helpful here to fill out a few details in this touching story of Jesus. Allow for an enlargement of the picture by the introduction of some truths about God and humanity found elsewhere in the Bible. With this composite image in hand, you can see that:

•(1) Coming home to God results in the unqualified forgiveness of all your past wrongs. The Father who has been waiting all this time does not want you to live in his presence with any regrets about the past. Previous mistakes are all forgiven and forgotten. It's a magical moment. It's the moment of your reconciliation with God. This moment happens once and need never be repeated. Without qualification you are received as a son or daughter by the Father.

What a moment filled with wonder when God forgives all the sinner's wrongdoing! All the errant ways of the past are forgotten. All the years of neglecting to give honour to the God of glory are forgiven. As far as the east is from the west, so far does he remove our transgressions from us.

Even the violations of God's law yet to be committed, if you can believe it, are pardoned in this once-in-a-lifetime moment. This interchange may seem to put God's integrity in a perilous position. But he is willing to take the risk, since his impeccable justice is retained because of the judgement endured by his Son in the sinner's place. His confidence in your future behaviour rests on his knowledge of the new life infused into you by his own Spirit.

Have you tasted the wonder of this magical moment? Do you know what it means to experience the reality of having the burden of guilt removed? Can you look boldly at the sins of your past, present and future with the confident knowledge that they never can condemn you before God again?

If it all seems too simple to be true, remember that the way for God's acceptance of sinners was a long time coming. God's Son was slain for sinners who had been 'chosen before the foundation of the world'.[1] Hundreds of years before Jesus accepted in himself the punishment that guilt-ridden sinners deserve, it was prophesied that this suffering servant of the Lord would be 'wounded for our transgressions', and 'bruised for our iniquities'.[2] It was stated that the just infliction of punishment for sinners would fall on him, and that with his stripes we would be healed. As one of Jesus' followers declared, 'He himself bore our sins in his own body on the tree'.[3]

No, it is not for nothing that this magical moment has come into the lives of people throughout the ages. God has done a wonderful thing in the surrendering of his Son. He has cleared the way for you to come home to God.

Come now in your spirit. Without taking a single step from where you are, you can come home to God. God is a spirit. In his total being as God he is always, everywhere present at the same time. Where you are he is. By the trusting outcry of your soul, you come home to him.

•(2) This magical moment when you come home to God also involves your being officially adopted as God's child. When the straying son returned, the waiting father instantly adorned him with all the insignia of sonship. He wrapped a festive robe about his shoulders. He placed the official signet ring of the family on his finger. He called for a great celebration.

The person who comes home to God in the name of Jesus receives a permanent imprint that he is a child of God, an heir of all his blessings, and a recipient of all his protection. The Father in heaven sends forth the Spirit of his Son into the heart of the believer. This all-powerful Holy Spirit seals the repentant sinner in his irreversible status as a son or daughter of God.

Have you experienced this reality of adoption into God's family? Can you embrace by faith the fact of your full reception by God as his own son? It's a vital part of the magical moment. It will make a permanent difference in the way you view everything that occurs in your life. Whether in triumph or in trial, you will see each circumstance of your life as being under the direction of his good will toward his own sons and daughters. Once you have grasped this reality, the magical moment of your coming home to God will shape the attitude you have toward every aspect of your life for evermore.

•(3) This magical moment of your coming home to God also will have a profound effect on your behaviour.

Previously you couldn't help it. Whenever you thought you could get away with it, you did exactly as your instincts dictated. You lusted, you lived for yourself. You gratified the desires of the flesh, and did exactly what you wanted.

Often the person who is not walking with God will make some effort to reform himself. He will try to patch up the little problem areas of his life. He determines to stop smoking. He will quit drinking too much. He will do his work more conscientiously at the office. He will be more careful about the kind of late-night TV shows he watches. But actually it's the life-style and the heart-direction behind that's the problem. His efforts to modify a few bad habits in life may be compared to the person who has fallen out of an airplane and is deeply concerned that the shoe on his left foot is wrongly laced.

When you come home to God, the entire pattern of your behaviour will change. It must. No longer will you live for your own self-interests. You will live for God and other people. The inner promptings that determine your decisions about life will come from the Spirit of God who has taken up residence within you. As the new 'inner agent' of your soul, God's Spirit will encourage you to please others rather than you. You will see to it that others get honour while you go unnoticed. Rather than seeking to get things out of people, you will give of yourself to them.

When a person comes home to God, everything changes. You are a new creation. Old things are passed away. All things become new. You will not regret this new life in Christ after your conversion. It will bless you, and make you a blessing to others.

If you have come home to God, you already know something of this change. The focus of your life has become quite different. It must be so.

Is it for you? Have you experienced the 'magical moment'? Do you know that all your sins have been forgiven by God? Has God's Spirit come to make the dead soul in you come to life? Can you see changes in your attitude and your behaviour that cannot be explained in any other way?

Is it not the greatest moment in your life?

It is!

Bible References

Reference 1 is found in
Ephesians chapter 1 verse 4
The translation is from the original text

Reference 2 is found in
Isaiah chapter 53 verse 5
NKJ translation

Reference 3 is found in
1 Peter chapter 2 verse 24
NIV translation

5

The Pilgrim's Progress

So everything in life is new! You have come home to God. You have been declared his adopted child. All your guilt for breaking your Maker's law is fully forgiven. You are regarded as righteous in his sight. All things are new, and you do everything differently.

Are all these things really true? Is everything actually different?

It is!!

Then what about the fact that you *still sin*?

You do, don't you? Despite all the talk about a totally new life, it isn't altogether new. You still covet the better look, the better life, the better car, house and salary of the other person. Their mind seems sharper than yours, and you covet their ability. Or the other person has a better position than you despite your superior training, experience and capabilities. So you simply cannot find it in yourself to remain content.

It's a problem – a very real problem. You say you are a
new person in Christ but you live with many of the same
old sins. You intend to put behind you anger, resentment,
lust of the flesh and doubts about God. But these things
keep cropping up in your soul, and you are deeply
saddened by their presence.

Don't feel you are alone in these matters. Don't think you
are the first person ever to struggle with indwelling sin,
despite your resolve to follow Christ. None less than the
apostle Paul had the same problem.

First Paul says, '...we have peace with God through our
Lord Jesus Christ'.[1] Since I have put my trust in his dying
for my sins, I have been declared by God to possess all his
righteousness. I cannot be condemned, despite the fact
that I have failed to live for God as I should. But then this
same Paul says, 'O wretched man that I am. Who will
deliver me from the body of this death?'[2]

He's miserable. Can you sense it?

What makes him so miserable?

He explains it. He says, *I sin!* That's what makes me so
miserable. 'For the thing that I would not do, that is
exactly what I do. And the very thing I want to do, that I
do not do.'[3]

What's going on? Can a person be miserable and feel
blessed at the same time?

Indeed he can. As a matter of fact, this tension-filled condition is a sure sign that you're making progress in your relation to God. If you are not miserable over your sin, then surely you are making no progress in your relationship to God. But a personal hatred of your sin clearly indicates that you are on the right way to serving God.

Making progress in this life with God may be compared to the experience of a pregnant woman. She's miserable in so many ways but at the same time she has that 'glow' about her. She feels so richly blessed. Her expectations are great because she knows God has planted life in her. She has an expectancy that supersedes all her many miseries. Every day, every month that passes means progress in the life that is maturing within her.

In a similar way, the person who has new life in Christ makes daily, weekly, monthly progress. A new life is taking shape in this person.

It's not an easy road. Sometimes it's two steps forward and one step back. Then at other times it's one step forward and two steps back. One day you restrain your tongue when someone provokes you. But two days later, when you least expect it, the old temper flares up again. One day the Bible comes alive for you as you read it. Your prayers soar heavenward like well-aimed arrows that hit the target every time. But the next day your sluggish mind can hardly launch a single wobbly arrow.

Don't despair over the slowness, the imperceptibility of your progress toward being conformed to the image of Christ. Moses, David, Peter and Paul all trudged along the same route. Moses lost his temper when he saw his nation dancing before the golden calf. David lost his purity when he gazed at the beauty of bathing Bathsheba. Peter lost (at least for a while) his right of leadership among the expanding Christian community when he shrunk from eating dinner at a table with Gentile converts. And Paul exclaimed, 'I see another law at work in the members of my body, waging war against the law of my mind and making me a prisoner of the law of sin at work within my members'.[4]

Nevertheless, give thanks for the struggle. Progress may be slow, even imperceptible to you. But it is not imperceptible to God. After all, who ever has been able to perceive his growth into maturity from one day to the next by checking daily in the mirror?

In the realm of the spirit, an additional factor makes your progress in getting closer to God seem like the slow steps of a pilgrim crossing the desert. The closer you get to God, the more aware you become of your personal shortcomings. Turning the lights ever brighter may make the reflection of your face in the mirror quite a bit clearer. But the brighter light also exposes more facial flaws. In the same way, while coming closer to Christ will empower you to give greater glory to God by your life, it also will humble you by uncovering previously hidden faults.

Yet this new awareness of your own imperfections, if viewed properly, can also serve as a sign of encouragement. For growth in humility is a basic ingredient in the development of the godly life. This growth in humility brings with it an awareness of the fact that the life lived for Christ is a gift of God's from beginning to end.

Can you honestly say you are on this pilgrim way? Remember, seeking to follow Jesus in self-sacrificing love is not the way to find forgiveness of sins and acceptance with God. Faith and faith alone, that attaches to the work of Jesus Christ for sinners, can save from the guilt of sin.

In a similar way, your progress in the pilgrim way that brings growth in conformity to Christ, also has faith and faith alone as its determining factor. Your determination of will can never enable you to overcome indwelling sin. It is the power of the resurrected Christ working in you that brings the prospect of redemption into the world of your realities. Looking in faith to him will empower your will to resist temptation more and more each day. Trusting in him will enable you to do the very specific good works that he has already planned for you to do.

Be encouraged as you traverse this pilgrim way. Join hands with all the other people around you that are going the same way. Rejoice in the fact that you now can reckon yourself to be dead to sins, but alive to God through Jesus Christ his Son.

Bible References

Reference 1 is found in
Romans chapter 5 verse 1
NIV version

Reference 2 is found in
Romans chapter 7 verse 24
The translation is from the original text

Reference 3 is found in
Romans chapter 7 verse 19
The translation is from the original text

Reference 4 is found in
Romans chapter 7 verse 23
NIV version

6
The Fullness of Joy

Can anything compare with the joy of discovery? An amateur astronomer was checking out the infinity of the night-sky. Suddenly his sight fixed on a heavenly body that never yet had been recorded. The discovery so excited him that he later said he feared he would die of a heart attack before he could have the heavenly body's existence recorded. His joy at the discovery almost paralyzed him.

Try to imagine the thrill that might come with a new discovery in God's great world. How exciting it would be to identify a new kind of butterfly, or a cure for the common cold, or another aspect of DNA.

Yet this kind of immeasurable joy over life can be the experience of the believer in Jesus Christ every day of his life. It can come in a variety of ways. But this newfound joy is all related to the life-giving Spirit of God that indwells a person from the moment of his being 'born from above'.

Remember the response of the two disciples travelling the road to Emmaus on the evening of Jesus' resurrection? Do you recall the effect their encounter with the risen Lord had on them? After Jesus had left them, one of the two unnamed disciples put the effect of their interchange in the form of a question: 'Did not our hearts *burn within us*...?'[1] Because of their meeting with the risen Christ along the road, they experienced a thrill beyond anything else they had ever known.

But what exactly was the source of their exhilaration? Was it the closeness to the resurrection body of their Lord? Was it the inestimable privilege of their eating a meal with Jesus? Was it the unforgettable instant when they first recognized that it was the crucified and risen Lord with whom they were conversing? No, it was none of these things that put the thrill into their souls.

One of these unnamed disciples identifies the source of their joy quite explicitly: 'Did not our hearts burn within us *when he opened to us the Scriptures?'*[2]

That's it! The opening of the Scriptures was the thing that caused their hearts to burn within them. As surprising as it may seem, it was not the presence of the resurrected Jesus in the flesh that thrilled them. For until the last moment of his being with them, 'their sight was restrained so that they did not recognize him.' Neither was it the startling moment of recognition that filled their hearts with such joy, although their witness that he had risen from the dead was most significant.

The thing that energized their lives was his opening of the Scriptures of the Old Testament to them. He taught them in all the Scriptures the things concerning himself, and for that reason their hearts were filled with joy and enthusiasm over life.

Why is this point so significant? It's significant because the nature of their experience is one that you can enjoy as well as they. You can experience this joy every day by constant communion with the living Christ. If those common, ordinary, everyday Christians could have their souls filled to the bursting-point as Jesus taught them in all the Scriptures the things concerning himself, then you can have the same revitalizing experience as well. The daily discovery of more and more of the riches of Christ your Saviour in the Scriptures can be, and should be, the vitalizing spark of freshness in your life every day. You have no need of seeing Jesus in the flesh in order to have your life revitalized. Just as the two disciples on the road to Emmaus came to know him through the Scriptures, so you can know him in his fullness and power by saturating yourself with God's word.

A second source of the fullness of joy comes through the fellowship of prayer. It's not just a matter of getting from God what you want when you want it. Though your needs may be very real (and your heavenly Father knows those real needs better than you), God must not be trivialized. The larger matter is that you live in constant communion and fellowship with him.

Through prayer you also know something of the joy of kindred spirits. Every now and then you just naturally 'click' with someone. You can talk about anything with them. You can work or recreate side by side with them for hours. Just being together lifts your spirit.

An even richer experience may be found through bonding with God. His Spirit and your spirit share in the deeper realities of life. When you face problems, conflicts, discouragements, his Spirit's presence provides inner encouragement. When all things are 'bright and beautiful', this same Spirit of God, with whom your spirit communes, enables you to direct your thanksgiving and praise in a way that honours him.

So your life takes on a legitimacy in all its expressions. A wholeness that encompasses all your different experiences comes to stay with you. It isn't that you're on the mountaintop of ecstatic experience all the time. That's a good thing, since you really wouldn't want to be always living on that exhausting level. But the instantaneous sharing of every aspect of life with the ever-present God, his Son and his Spirit, makes you ever more aware of the breadth, the length, the depth and the height of the love of God that surpasses human comprehension. It's this ever-present joy deep down within that makes all of life so meaningful.

A third source of this fullness of joy is the challenge of sacrificial service to Christ. A person, even a person with the lowest of metabolisms, can endure only so much sitting around doing nothing. Sometimes perpetual idleness sounds great, especially to the overburdened. But the actual experience can quickly become quite boring.

But your new life in Christ never will become a drag, for God has too many things for you to do. To everyone who believes in him he has a special commission. He has some work cut out for you, and your joy will be multiplied as your surrender yourself as one enslaved to serve him.

Imagine that you were a distinctively shaped piece of a jigsaw puzzle. You start off the day in a jumbled pile dumped out of a box. For a while you 'sit on the sidelines' while lots of other people are being put into their proper places. But finally your turn comes. The 'master maker' picks you up and places you snugly in conjunction with other puzzle pieces. As you find yourself linked together with them, you discover that your distinctive colour, shape and size all make sense. You find fulfilment in realizing your purpose in life.

Obviously all illustrations are defective, and the idea of your being like a single piece of a jigsaw puzzle has many inherent defects. Life on this planet in conjunction with many variables is much more complicated that that. You don't have just one place, one shape, one job.

Yet the illustration embodies an important truth. You as a human being have a certain size, shape and purpose in God's plan. As a matter of fact, every day he wants you to achieve certain purposes that will contribute to his larger, all-encompassing plan. This day he may want you to share the gospel with a stranger. Next he would have you write a letter of encouragement to your friend in need. Still again, he may intend that you, given your present circumstance, should read a book, plant a garden, or practise a musical instrument. But the wonder of it all is the joy, the sense of fulfilment that comes with whatever you do, so long as it is done in faith, to his glory, and according to his commands. It's the work of his vitalizing Spirit in you once more.

A special joy will come as you uncover the distinctive gifts God has given you for serving in his kingdom and his church. Jesus Christ, from the vantage-point of his throne in heaven, has poured out his Holy Spirit on men and women, young and old, Jew and non-Jew. As a believer in Christ, you are a benefactor of these spiritual gifts for service.

As you evaluate your own abilities to serve in God's world by the power of God's Spirit, don't think in stagnant terms. Each new situation in your life may bring with it new gifts for serving your Lord.

In the realm of birds, there are the ground-hoppers, the bush-hoppers, and sky-soarers. The ground-hoppers look for the bugs and worms of the grass. The bush-hoppers pluck the berries from the garden greenery. The sky-soarers survey the total terrain for their nourishment.

In a similar way, different people are assigned different tasks and domains. Some tasks may seem more humble,

some more exalted. But the joyful spirit of the servant of
God will find fullness and contentment whatever his
currently assigned task might be.

Of course, it must be recognized that serving the righteous
cause of God in an unrighteous world inevitably means
suffering at the hands of sinners. Always some will misun-
derstand you, misinterpret your motives, and seek to stop
whatever you are doing in the name of God. For 'all who
will live godly in Christ Jesus shall suffer persecution'.[3] Only
with 'many hardships' shall a person enter the kingdom of
God. You cannot, you must not, be so naive that you are
surprised by the 'fiery trials' that come on you, as though
some strange thing had happened to you, as though it
were something that never before had happened to the
people of God.

Instead of being surprised, you must allow the spirit of
your newfound joy to embrace these experiences as well.
However they come, they can benefit you and give glory
to God.

A fourth source of abundant joy will be found in the act of
worshipping God with all your soul in the temple of the
new covenant. In the final state of things, worshipping God
will be the highlight of heaven. But you need not wait.
When you come to church for worship, you meet with the
Father, the Son and the Spirit. They all are present to make
themselves personally known to you. As the Word of God
is read and its message preached, the Lord himself offers
encouragement, consolation and admonition. As you sing,

pray and present your offerings, you join with the heavenly host and the multitude of the redeemed that form in themselves the living temple where God dwells. Together you experience the exhilarating joy of honouring the God who is your Maker and Redeemer. As you participate in the ceremony of baptism and the Lord's Supper, you find strength for your soul through intimate fellowship with the triune God. Worshipping God in the living temple of the new covenant quickly becomes a source of constant rejuvenation and joy.

So the prize of abundant joy in life is yours for the seizing. With full awareness of the fact that all strength and energy for doing God's will comes from the Spirit of Christ, give yourself over to the doing of his will. As he reveals himself in his Word, as you commune with his person, as you make full use of your abilities to serve him, you will discover the immeasurable joys of life.

Bible References

References 1 & 2 are found in
Luke chapter 24 verse 32
The translation is from the original text

Reference 3 is found in
2 Timothy chapter 3 verse 12
The translation is taken from the original text

7

The Maturing Years

Maturity is not necessarily a function of age. Some young Christians still in their teenage years may be quite mature in their spiritual development. At the same time, some people may be greying at the temples, but you never would guess their age by the level of spiritual maturity that they display.

Maturity may be associated with sobriety. Rather than viewing life through illusionary glasses that distort colours and shapes, the mature person sees things as they really are. As a consequence, the mature Christian is not so easily thrown off balance by the collapse of a venture of faith, or by the betrayal of a close friend. At the same time, a person that has matured properly in Christ derives more contentment from life than other people with less inner stability.

Maturity of years in age (not necessarily the same as maturity of years in Christ) brings with it both dangers and blessings. One pitfall that passing years can bring is a seed of scepticism. Even though the faith continues to be affirmed, a growing residue of uncertainty about the realities of faith lies just beneath the surface of the soul. Because of repeated disappointments over seemingly legitimate expectations, a person may train himself to look for less in terms of the mighty acts of God. A person living with the seed of scepticism in his soul will be a little slower to speak out for the cause of Christ. Having had his fingers burned in the past because he was a little too anxious to take up the cause, he is more inclined to let things pass.

But scepticism is not the only option for a person maturing in Christian experience. Paul the Apostle had many disappointments. He had to endure the desertion of John Mark, which later led to a heated dispute with the genial Barnabas. He had to rebuke Peter publicly face-to-face because of his shameful scorning of Gentile believers. He had to denounce his pharisaic brothers who had become believers because they tried to force Gentile converts to be circumcised. He had no option other than to address the Galatian church as 'foolish' because they had turned so quickly to 'another' gospel. He had to excommunicate a member of the Corinthian church because the church itself would not assume its proper responsibility. In the final stage of his life as an old man in a cold prison, he had to say, 'At my first defence, no one came to my support, but everyone deserted me.'[1]

If anyone ever had cause for scepticism, it was the Apostle Paul. One disappointment after another dogged his tracks.

But a proper maturing in Christ will not be thrown off by these temporary disappointments. God's gospel is the standard by which all reality must be judged. His commitment of 'all authority' to the resurrected Christ is not threatened by the fickleness of human beings. So Paul's testimony throughout his life serves as a ringing affirmation of the unshaken confidence he has in Christ. He is persuaded that '...neither death nor life nor angels nor principalities nor powers, nor things present nor things to come...shall be able to separate us from the love of God that is in Christ Jesus our Lord.'[2] Never will the Apostle be distracted from asserting 'I know whom I have believed, and am persuaded that he is able to keep that which I have committed to him until that day'.[3] That's maturity! Its measure is found in the calm assurance that supersedes all potential discouragements, and goes on to the end holding forth the banner of an unswerving faith that is sure to inspire the generations to come.

Another test of the maturing years arises as a consequence of personal achievement in the service of Christ. In younger years, generally the breath is knocked out of a self-sufficient person by being 'put in his place' through the embarrassment that comes from failure. But over time, position, success and recognition can go to a person's head and heart. It might be assumed that an older person would be able to recognize the seed of pride in his heart and deal with it. But more times than might be imagined the reverse is true. The man of accomplishment becomes accustomed to having others defer to his way and his will.

His growing sense of power in himself makes him expect that all 'lesser men' will move aside, showing him the respect he rightly has earned.

So good king Uzziah, a man of many achievements who also 'loved the soil', expected Israel's priesthood to step aside when he assumed to himself the privilege of offering incense in the temple. But while ranting and raging at the priests for their resistance, leprosy sprung out in his forehead. To the day of his death he had to bear that very public mark of God's humiliation of his pride.[4]

How different is David as he departs the capitol city of Jerusalem in order to avoid a bloody confrontation with the advancing troops of his rebellious son Absolam. While in the humiliation of flight, David patiently bows his head and bears the abuses of Shimei his servant. How those curses, those hurled stones and dirt-clogs must have stung the heart of the king. But he bore it all like the mature man of God that he was. God had sent this scoffer, and God would have to be the one to defend the cause of the king when he saw fit.

Pride is one of the major pitfalls that can swallow up those who have achieved some level of greatness over the years. It is as though they consume themselves in attempting to maintain their own self-dignity.

But contrary to the standards of the world, there is another way for the truly mature to react both to their 'good days' and their 'bad days'. They can cultivate the mind of Christ. He was in his very essence God. Yet he humbled himself, scorned the shame of the cross, and in the end received a greater glory than any other man.

The challenge is yours. The years will quickly pass. You may become foolishly proud as you grow older. Or you may follow the wiser way and be happy for the Lord to treat you as a child.

On the positive side, maturing in Christ may bring with it many benefits. You may find it much easier to take setbacks in your stride. Even large-scale losses will not deter your moving onward and upward toward the goal of Christlikeness. For you will have come to understand that 'being' is more important than 'doing'. 'Being' the right person before God is much more important than 'doing' certain noteworthy things.

In addition, maturity in Christ should find you quite capable of closing your ears to the harping voices of criticism. Obviously it is most important to be able to learn from legitimate criticism, and to make the proper mid-course corrections. But at the same time there is great wisdom in the saying of Qohelet, better known as the 'preacher,' in Ecclesiastes:

'Do not pay attention to every word people say,
or you may hear your servant cursing you-
for you know in your heart
that many times you yourself have cursed others'.[5]

If you're too busy listening to what people say about you, then you will accomplish little that lasts for God. Did Jesus not teach this clearly enough? The broad way followed by the majority leads to self-destruction. The narrow way may involve a lonely crucifixion, since two people cannot hang on the same cross. But watch and see. The narrower road with fewer people eventually leads to life eternal. A mature perspective on life will recognize the truth of Jesus' words.

At the same time, a maturing in wisdom will show you how to be at peace with your enemies. It won't happen always, and it never will be a perfect peace. But an old adage speaks volumes in terms of personal relations with those who oppose you:

> Love and I had a wit (will) to win;
> We drew a circle that took him in.
> > from *Outwitted* by Edwin Markham

Jesus said it even better:

'Love your enemies, do good to them, and lend to them without expecting to get anything back. Then your reward will be great, and you will be sons of the Most High, because he is kind to the ungrateful and wicked.'[6]

Some people may regard you as their enemy. But don't you regard them as your enemy. It's the mature perspective on life that some people never understand. But you would do well to learn it before too many years go by.

Finally, maturity in Christ will teach you to hold material possessions loosely. Don't tighten your grip on things. Otherwise *rigor mortis* will set in, and you may never be able to let go. Jesus taught it so clearly:

'Lay not up for yourselves treasures on earth'.[7]
'Take heed and beware of covetousness'.[8]
'God said to him, "You fool! This very night your very life will be demanded of you. Then who will get what you have prepared for yourself?"'[9]

The mature person is not the one who finally has enough money banked away to enable him to retire comfortably. The mature person is the one who has stored up treasures in heaven.

The mature in Christ will not allow themselves even to be captured by the material comforts of this life. A house, a car, a wardrobe, a vacation are to him gifts from God that he can enjoy so long as they are available. But his happiness in life is never dependent on them. How liberating it is to be content with the things you have, and to labour so that you will have a little extra to give to others.

So maturing in Christ may not take you where you want to go. But if you are trusting him, the passing of years will take you where you ought to be. The deepening of life in Christ is a precious thing, worth more than anything else in this world. Seek it first, and all other needs will be met as well.

Reference 1 is found in
2 Timothy chapter 4 verse 16
NIV translation

Reference 2 is found in
Romans chapter 8 verse 38
NKJ translation

Reference 3 is found in
2 Timothy chapter 1 verse 12
The translation is from the original text

Reference 4 is found in
2 Kings chapter 15 verses 1-7.
King Uzziah is also called Azariah

Reference 5 is found in
Ecclesiastes chapter 7 verses 21-22
NIV translation

Reference 6 is found in
Matthew chapter 5 verse 44
The translation is from the original text

Reference 7 is found in
Matthew chapter 6 verse 19
The translation is from the original text

Reference 8 is found in
Luke chapter 12 verse 15
NIV translation

Reference 9 is found in
Luke chapter 12 verses 20-21
The translation is from the original text

Bible References

8
Turning Time into Eternity

As a person matures in years, his thoughts naturally turn to time as it relates to eternity. Is there such a thing as eternity? Does it have meaning to me? Or is the existence of a human being encapsulated exclusively in the sequence of days and years that are designated as 'time'?

Generally time is thought of in terms of the here and the now, while eternity is defined in relation to the then and there. This very common distinction may be a major source of the scepticism about eternity, for it is rather difficult to believe in something you never have experienced.

But as distantly related as time and eternity may appear, they actually are quite closely intertwined. For eternity has been compressed into time. 'Eternal life' refers not merely to the *duration* of a person's existence; it describes just as significantly the *quality* of a person's existence. By receiving God's gift of eternal life, the qualities of reality that characterize eternity become embodied in time.

If this kind of relation between ever-present time and seemingly distant eternity is difficult to grasp, consider the relation of our little planet earth and its mother-star, the sun, to the vast array of heavenly bodies known as the 'milky way.' Above us are millions, billions of stars that give the appearance of a thin haze stretching across the breadth of the night sky. Astronomers explain that the nearest star-neighbour to our own solar system is about twenty-six trillion miles away from earth.

Yet it is a fact that our sun, along with this planet earth, actually is a part of the 'milky way'! Though the haze above appears to be so far away, we actually are enveloped in the mist of that host of innumerable stars.

In a similar way, eternity may seem a stranger because of its apparent distance from the realities of time and space. But one of God's great miracles is to put eternity into time. The essential realities that stretch into the endless future can be known in this fleeting moment of 'now'.

The Apostle Paul talks about the realities of eternity as they are manifest in time. In a classic chapter of the Bible, he says, 'And now abide faith, hope and love; these three'.[1] When Paul says these qualities 'abide', he means they partake of the nature of eternity. They continue forever just because in their essence they characterize eternity as God the Creator has designed it.

Hatred will not continue in the presence of God forever. He will not allow it. He will consign all hatred to the pit of hell. But love will remain. For God is love.

Unbelief has no long-life characteristics. It will be banished with the unbeliever. But belief, faith, entrusting oneself to God the Redeemer, is an act that is guaranteed to remain forever. For faith, the ability to believe, is a gift graciously granted by God himself.

Living without hope cannot survive, for hopelessness is self-destructive. A person who lives without hope cannot hope to live long, for hope in its very essence characterizes eternity.

So one of the great challenge of life is to turn time into eternity. Somehow the qualities that mark off eternal realities must inject themselves into time. But how?

It cannot be that time will be turned into eternity through escapism. Many religions have proposed just that procedure. If a person can disentangle himself from the realm of time and space, then perhaps he can experience the transforming realities of eternity. But since you cannot escape from yourself as a creature of time and space, no amount of withdrawal from the world in which you live can free you from the 'who', the 'when' and the 'where' that you are. Neither hallucinatory drugs nor mystical trances can arrest the ever-onward ageing process of the real 'you'.

The intrusion of eternity into time may best be understood by considering two historical events: the incarnation of the Son of God and the outpouring of the Spirit of God. These two moments in history have changed forever the realm of the world in which we humans live.

By the incarnation the eternal God infused the realities of eternity into time. It would not have been thought possible until it happened. But 'in the fullness of time' God sent forth his Son into this world. He was fully man, but he had in himself the very essence of God. He commanded wind and waves, he multiplied loaves and fishes, he raised the dead to life. Yet he suffered hunger, sleeplessness, and exhaustion. He was so wounded in spirit that he wept. He was subjected to trial (a mock trial), he received the sentence of death (although declared innocent by his judge), and he died the cruel death of the cross (yet it was he who 'gave up his spirit'). By the resurrection of his body, he broke the bonds of man's last great enemy, which is the silent spectre of death. Now he forever lives as the reigning sovereign of the world. At the right time he shall be manifested for what he already is – the King of the kings and the Lord of the lords. In the end, the exercise of his power shall set all things straight, and the merger of time with eternity will be perfected.

But already he has brought 'eternal life' into time. Already you can experience the realities of eternity within the confines of time. You can experience now the wonders of God's working that lasts forever.

A second great moment in history when eternity was injected into time occurred at the outpouring of God's Spirit by the exalted Son of God. This unique gift of God had been promised long before. The coming of the Spirit of God was, as a matter of fact, *the* promise. In his coming all the promises of God receive initial realization as well as positive confirmation.

Remember that the Spirit of God is no less than the totality of the infinite God himself. By his coming to set up permanent residence within a finite human being, eternity becomes resident in time. Once that has happened, the lifestyle of the human being is forever transformed. All things mundane and temporal now have the potential of being infused with the characteristics of eternity.

So now it is possible to talk concretely about 'turning time into eternity'. For even in the everyday life of commonplace people like you and me, it happens. It happens, not by an escape from the world of space and time as we know it, but by a transformation of the world itself.

Consider for instance the potency of 'faith, hope and love' as elements that abide for eternity. Think about how these three aspects of eternity can change the things of time.

By *faith* you can accept your present situation in life as something appointed by God for your good. Whether married or single, in school or out, at home or away, you can trust your present situation to be the sovereign appointment of the eternal God. At the same time by faith you can step out into an entirely different world than that to which you are currently accustomed. In either case, the simple act of faith transforms your circumstance so that every experience in life becomes a source of blessing to yourself as well as to others, simply because by faith you realize that God is in it.

And then there's *hope*. Paul says that hope abides forever. But in what sense can it be said that hope abides in eternity? Is there anything a person might 'hope for' throughout the endless ages of eternity? Should it not be expected that at the point of entering the life to come, he would receive from God's hand whatever blessing he might expect, rather than perpetually hoping for something yet to come?

The reference in Scripture to the eternal continuation of hope suggests something else. Expectancy will not end when life in heaven begins. Since God is infinite in all his attributes, you may anticipate an ever-increasing aware-ness of His glories. Because of his greatness, there can be no limit to the ecstasies in coming to know him better and better.

If hope abides for eternity, then let hope characterize every moment of time. Because of the hope that Christ brings, the lonely, the jobless, the hungry, the diseased, the depressed can forever look forward to the better day that is sure to come. So you may live with unlimited expecta-tion regarding the way God is yet to display his love, his power, his compassion, his personal presence. Let today's troubles be transformed into a spur of expectation by an abiding hope.

Finally there is *love*. The greatest of these things that abide for eternity is love. Frustration over the temporality of life need not remain where there is love. For love possesses the greatest potential for turning time into eternity.

Two Christian medical students came down from the mountains of Peru to prepare themselves for service. In those days, the philosophy of communism was tearing the country apart. These two young men had a vision. Their intent was to become trained as medical doctors. They would return to the poor people of the mountain regions of Peru and display the love of Christ by caring for the needs of their own people for little or no pay. In this manner they would show that Christianity was greater than communism.

As students they lived in spartan circumstances. Their apartment had hardly a chair for sitting. But on the mantelpiece of their living room was a single object, a piece of art in the form of a man moulded from baked clay. Nothing else adorned the room. When a Christian visitor came, one of the men reached out to the mantle, took down the object of art, and placed it in the stranger's hands. 'Take it', he said. 'Let it serve as a remembrance, so you never will forget us.'

In one instant, by this single gesture, time was turned into eternity. Their unselfish lives of love now became embodied in that single object of art. The cords of love bound the one-time visitor to these young men forever. 'The greatest of these', which is love, had transformed a moment of time into eternity.

So now it's your turn. As you read right now of this simple event that occurred in a distant land many years ago, you may be the instrument of extending the ripples of its influence into future decades. You may determine at this moment to participate in the process that is going on all about you. You too may turn the things of time into the values of eternity.

Bible References

Reference 1 is found in
1 Corinthians chapter 13 verse 13
NKJ translation

9

Confronting the End – And the Beginning

Mankind began his journey through time and eternity at home with God. Now the time has come for returning home to God.

Some people find this life to be so filled with misery and disappointment that they wish it could end soon. This 'wearisome way' may seem to be leading nowhere for you.

This life will have its end soon enough. But in the meantime, nothing could be better than living out your days with the knowledge that God your loving heavenly Father has planned your way for you. Despite all your troubles and the inevitability of the end that is before you, a life of joyful service can be yours from this day forward.

A young minister, having just completed many years of schooling designed to prepare him for serving others, learned of a nearby need. The older man in the house across the road had been bedridden, waiting for death for over twenty years. So the young man decided to go and offer a cheering word.

In the bedroom he saw what only could be described as a human vegetable. This man lay on his back, completely immobile from his neck down. His entire body consisted of pale, flabby flesh. For days, months, years, decades he had lived in this condition. His circumstance must have made him think continually of the value of eternity. He had lived constantly in the face of death. He obviously had need for a word of consolation and comfort.

But before the young minister could speak, the invalid seized the opportunity to say his own word of consolation and encouragement. Out of a heart filled with the richness of God's grace, this man's mouth overflowed with precious treasures of truth he had discovered in God's word. Though totally confined to bed, this man had been filled to overflowing through constant communion with God his loving Father. The youthful minister had come with the good intention of leaving a blessing behind. But in the end he left as the one who had been abundantly blessed. For this man had conquered the prospect of death by his faith in the ever-living God.

Of course it must be recognized that there is a final going home to God, and people must prepare for that transition. Jesus himself, on the night before his death, had home-coming on his mind. He spoke of the 'many mansions' in his Father's house. He encouraged his followers to live without fear because he was going to prepare a place for them. But in the anticipation of a future homecoming, don't forget that by entrusting your life to Jesus you have already come home to God. Even now you may expect to be full of the good things that come by his grace.

So a balance must be sought. Paul summarized the healthy perspective of the person that feels at home with God. He was prepared at any moment to depart this life and to be with Christ, which he declared to be 'far better' than enjoying the greatest blessings that could be imagined in this life. At the same time, his appointment by Christ as an 'Apostle to the Gentiles' gave his current life great significance in terms of good for others. So while always aware of the benefits of the final homecoming, he did not know whether he would prefer to remain in this present life or to pass on into the life to come.

It's a good situation to be in. You can't lose, no matter how difficult may be your present circumstance. You may look with anticipation toward the future entrance into your heavenly Father's home. At the same time, you may find rich meaningfulness in every experience of this life because you have already 'come home' to God.

Many men of old have shown the way. The last thing Jacob wanted to do was to leave the land God had promised him. Some people have even suggested that Jacob made a great mistake in leaving Canaan for Egypt in order to escape the famine. They conclude that many troubles came to him just because he wandered outside the borders of the land designated by God for him. But God clearly told Jacob not to worry about going down to Egypt. So he went although he always intended to go back. God promised at the time of his departure from the land of promise that he would return.

So Jacob made his preparations. If he could not live out his life in the land of promise, then he must be buried there. He made his son swear that when he died he would be returned to the land God had promised him, a land that he never had possessed.

That time eventually came. After the manner of the Egyptians, the patriarch Jacob was embalmed. Accompanied by a royal Egyptian entourage, the body of Jacob was returned to the land that God had promised him. He was laid to rest in the cave of Machpelah, located in Hebron at the far end of the plot that Abraham had acquired for his wife Sarah's burial almost two hundred years earlier.

So there he rests. He waits. He never received the fulfilment of God's promises.[1]

But the unchanging God cannot and will not lie. One day his promise shall be fulfilled. The place of Jacob's end will prove to be the place of his new beginning. As the closing down of this present world order comes to pass, so the opening of the new order will begin. The new heavens and the new earth will welcome all who are in Christ to their eternal dwelling. In the new order they shall live forever in the Father's eternal home as prepared by Jesus Christ.

It's a good time for you to make your preparations right now. It's a good thing to confront the end, and to see it in terms of the new beginning. Just as Jacob seized the promise of God and would not let it go, so you can claim by faith the promises of Jesus. You can come home to God through faith in him. You can live eternally with God through him. You can find fullness of life in him.

Bible References

Reference 1 is found in
Genesis chapter 50 verses 1-14

10

The Eternal Plan Revisited

So God has a plan. His plan is eternal, stretching from eternity past and reaching into eternity future. Included in his plan is a way to bring people home to himself.

People also make their plans. With strength of will they set themselves on a certain course. All too often the plans of people point in a direction that is counter to the purposes of God. People like to think of themselves as self-determining. No one or no thing will overthrow their plans.

In this way men set themselves against God. It has been this way from the beginning. But no plan of man can thwart the purposes of God. For 'he does as he will in the armies of heaven and among the inhabitants of earth; and no one can restrain his hand or say to him, "What are you doing?"'[1]

The supremacy of the eternal plan of God supersedes the temporal purposes of men, and for that fact we may be thankful. For his plan includes a determination to 'bring many sons to glory.'[2] In order to accomplish this goal,

Jesus the eternal Son of God was made like man in every way, and yet without the inherent stain of sin that has marred the basic nature of every other human being that has ever lived. He is a unique person. If his coming to save sinners had not been a central feature in the eternal plan, no human being ever would have come home to God.

You may be among those who have heard the irresistible call of God. You may have become weary of following your own way. Life seems hollow – sometimes even cruel. The call of God has spoken to your heart. You cannot be content until you have come back to him. By responding to his call you come home at last. This coming back to God actually wasn't your plan; it was his plan.

You will not be alone if you come home to God. Left to themselves, no one would return to God because of their hardened hearts. But the eternal plan of God will see to it that many people will come home to him. According to his appointment, their own plans will be submerged in his eternal purpose.

So in the end the house of God shall be full. Many people will come from east and west, from north and south. They will sit down with the ancients of old at the banquet table of God. There they will dine with Abraham and Moses. There they will feast alongside Bathsheba the mother of King Solomon and Mary the mother of King Jesus.

In the days when the winds of revival swept across America, churches would often hold 'protracted' meetings. The visiting messenger sent from God would stay for days. Everyone would gather from far and wide to enjoy the singing, the preaching, the testifying, the fellowshipping. People would enjoy the time together so much that the meeting would be 'protracted' or 'prolonged' for days without end.

A major part of every 'protracted' meeting would be 'dinner on the grounds'. The best cooks of the county would stir up a meal of fried chicken, corn casserole, beans, tomatoes, okra, pies and cakes. It was a grand old time of enjoying all the bounties of God's grace.

So shall it be when the eternal plan of God comes to its climax. Those who have come home to him will sit down at the wedding feast of the Lamb. Angelic messengers will declare the eternal gospel. Sacred choirs will sing 'Worthy is the Lamb that was slain....'[3] Multitudes from every nation will rejoice at their welcome into the heavenly home. The whole of creation will shout, 'Hallelujah! For the Lord God Omnipotent Reigns.'[4]

So the eternal plan will find its fulfilment. The sovereign God will see to it. His house shall be filled.

You have an open door before you. You have a personal invitation to come home to God. Return to him today, and the way will be made clear for you to enjoy heaven's eternal home.

You gain nothing by delay. Come home to God-today.

Bible References

Reference 1 is found in
Daniel chapter 4 verse 35
The translation is from the original text

Reference 2 is found in
Hebrews chapter 2 verse 10
NIV translation

Reference 3 is found in
Revelation chapter 5 verse 12
The translation is from the original text

Reference 4 is found in
Revelation chapter 19 verse 6
NKJ translation

Other titles by O. Palmer Robertson published
by Evangelical Press

Prophet Of The Coming Day
Welwyn Commentary Series on Joel

Psalms In Congregational Celebration
Studies of twenty-five psalms

A wide range of excellent books on spiritual subject is available from Evangelical Press. Please write to us for your free catalogue or contact us by e-mail.

Evangelical Press
Faverdale North Industrial Estate, Darlington, DL3 OPH, England

Evangelical Press USA
PO Box 825, Webster, New York 14580, USA

e-mail sales: sales@evangelicalpress.org

web: http://www.evangelicalpress.org